AF601412

Denise Shick

The Boy Who Liked Tea Parties

Illustrated by Yana Popova

Joey and Jill live next to each other.

Joey likes to go to Jill's house.
She has lots of toys.
Jill likes to play with her dolls.
Joey likes to dress the dolls
in their fancy clothes.

Sometimes Joey, Jill, and the dolls have a tea party.
They eat sugar cookies and put spoonfuls of honey in their tea.

Jill wears a fancy hat
and lots of colorful beads.
Joey puts on a hat and beads too.
They laugh as they make faces
in the mirror and
dance around the room.

One night at dinner, Dad asked,
"What did you do today?"
"I played with Jill."
"Did you have fun?"

"Sure. We had a tea party and wore fancy hats. Jill's mom makes yummy cookies."
Dad was quiet. His neck turned red, and he looked mad. Joey looked over at Mom. She looked down at her plate. Her cheeks were red.

The next afternoon, Joey asked Mom, "Can I play with Jill today?"
"What about Billy?" she said. "Would you like to play with him today?"
Joey frowned. "I like playing with Jill better."
"But won't it be fun to play with another boy?"
"I guess."

After Mom took Joey to Billy's house,
the boys went out to the backyard.
Billy had a large sandbox filled with dump trucks
and track hoes and cranes.
"Let's see how big of a hole we can dig," Billy said.
"Okay." The sun grew hot as they scooped and dumped.

Joey said, "How about we go inside and get some juice and cookies?"
"No," said Billy. "My baby brother is taking a nap.
My mom says we need to stay outside."

That night at dinner, Dad asked Joey,
"Did you have fun at Billy's today?"
"It was okay, I guess."
"Why such a sad face?" Dad asked.

"I have more fun with Jill."
Joey looked at Dad, then Mom.
They looked at each other.

The next afternoon when Joey got home from school,
Dad's car was parked in the driveway.
What, Joey wondered, *is Dad doing home from work?*

When Joey entered the kitchen
for his after-school snack,
Dad said, “Come on, Joey.
Today is Dad and Son Day.
We’re going on an adventure.”

First, Joey and Dad stopped at the ice cream shop. They each ordered a scoop of chocolate-chip ice cream with whipped cream and a cherry.

Then they went to the toy store. Joey picked out two GI Joe dolls and a jeep they could ride in.

Finally, Joey and Dad went to a used clothing store.
They both tried on funny shirts and hats.

Joey picked out a bright blue shirt with pineapples and flowers on it.
He also found a black hat with green sparkly sequins on it.
Dad said, "That hat is called a bowler." They both laughed.

At bedtime, Dad read a Bible story about Joseph.
His father gave him a special colorful coat. Later in the story,
Joseph had to dress up like an Egyptian
in a fancy robe and a sparkly hat.

"God made me a boy," Dad said as he closed the book.
"God made you a boy." He tapped Joey's nose. "Boys are special. Some of us like trucks and dirt. Some of us like sparkly hats and tea parties."
Dad smoothed the covers and stood.

"I'm glad you have friends like Billy and Jill. It's okay to play dress-up and have tea parties with Jill. It's okay to play trucks with Billy. But always remember that God made you a boy. He loves the boy that you are, and so do I."

Dad walked over to Joey's desk, laid down the book, and picked up the new hat. He put it on his head, waved his hands, and made a silly face. Joey laughed.

"You should come to Jill's house and dance with us."

"Maybe I will."

honey

THE END

For Parents:

If you want to read more about Joseph, his story is recorded in Genesis 37, 39–50. If your son struggles with his identity as a boy, here are some Scripture passages that may help him understand that God gives every boy different skills and interests, which can all be used to serve God.

Psalm 139:14–16 affirms that God designed every part of him—both his appearance and interests. He is a one-of-a-kind masterpiece.

Jeremiah 1:5 affirms that God has a purpose for him and has given him the interests and abilities he needs to become the boy God designed him to be.

Genesis 25:27, 29 indicates that Jacob enjoyed cooking and indoor activities while his twin brother, Esau, enjoyed hunting and other outdoor activities. God chose Jacob to become the father of twelve sons. Their descendants became the nation of Israel.

Exodus 28:3–4 describes the skilled fabric designers and weavers who made fancy clothing for the priests. The artistic abilities of these men were a gift from God.

Exodus 31:1–11 introduces Bezalel, Oholiab, and other craftsman who were filled with the Spirit of God and able to create all kinds of beautiful objects—furniture, jewelry, bowls, and fabrics. These works of art were used in God's house. (Also see Exodus 35:30–35, 36:8, and 37:29.)

First Samuel 16:18 describes David as a young man who was both a warrior and a musician. Many of the songs he wrote are in the book of Psalms, including Psalm 8 and Psalm 23. His songs still help God's people express their praise and thanksgiving.

Second Samuel 6:14–15 records that David, and many others, danced before the Lord as an act of worship.

First Chronicles 15:16–19 lists some of the hundreds of singers and musicians David appointed to lead worship. Their instrumental music and songs helped people praise God. Also see 2 Chronicles 5:11–12.

Endorsements

I am really impressed by Denise Shick's book, *The Boy Who Liked Tea Parties.*

As a psychiatrist in private practice for more than three decades serving the LGBT families, I have met a lot of parents who do not know what to do when they find their children expressing transgenderism or are gender nonconforming. Most of these parents reproach their children for their transgender desires, behavior, or identity and coerce them to be gender conforming; others may adopt a wait-and-see approach and refrain from doing anything, hoping that the child is just passing through a phase. Both responses are far from satisfactory, for the former response might further jeopardize the parent-child relationship, making the child more miserable, and the latter response misses the opportunity for early intervention and care for the needy transgender child.

I cannot agree more with Denise's proposed healthy and balanced way of parenting transgender children. First, do not to fall into the trap of gender stereotypes. Second, parents can still love and accept their children despite disapproval of their behaviors. Third, strengthen the father-son emotional bonding and modeling. Fourth, rather than reproaching or reinforcing the child's transgender behavior, affirm the child's sexual identity in a gentle, loving way. Fifth, co-parenting is essential because parents have to cooperate and be united.

I highly recommend Denise's book to all parents who would like to help their children develop psychosexual health and gender confidence.

Dr. Kwai-Wah Hong
Specialist in Psychiatry
M.B.,B.S.(H.K.), M.R.C.Psych.(U.K.), F.H.K.C.Psych.
Founder of Post Gay Alliance and Hong Kong Psychosexual Education Association

Thank you, Denise, for turning your personal pain into hope for families!

Transgenderism is a very complex and politicized topic, and I am so proud of Denise for filling in the gaps of healthy gender identity development that academia has ignored but used as a political tool for the advancement of an ideology without scientific evidence.

Your courage in authoring children's books on the subject is laudable, and you have set a role model for us. No, to be helpful you don't necessarily have to have an academic credential because your personal experience is the best firsthand knowledge that can help parents in a child's healthy gender formation and development. Everyone who is interested in child development should make their knowledge base complete by reading and using the work of Denise Shick!

The concepts and content of this volume are age appropriate as well as clinically healthy: that is, often early gender identity development in children is solely based on the intimate emotional and social relationship with the same-sex parent—father and son, mother and daughter. This book gives readers some ideas on how parents can first be aware of gender non-compliance in children and how parents can lovingly and naturally meet the gender developmental needs of their children without the involvement of mental health professionals. Thank you, Denise, for this book to make prevention a possibility and a reality!

I strongly recommend all new parents (especially dads) have book-study small groups so they can benefit from Denise Shick's contribution to effective parenting skills early, in a preventive effort, so our children can be given a chance to grow up with healthy gender confidence. All culture-informed leaders should be interested in healthy gender development, and I recommend you read Denise Shick's other titles, which are equally excellent!

Melvin Wong, Ph.D.
Licensed Clinical Psychologist, California
Former assistant professor of psychiatry, UCSF
Former Honorary Director: Pastoral Counseling Program,
Hong Kong Baptist Theological Seminary

The Boy Who Liked Tea Parties

Book Design: Yana Popova
First Edition

ISBN: 978-1-7365951-1-4

www.ingramcontent.com/pod-product-compliance
Ingram Content Group UK Ltd.
Pitfield, Milton Keynes, MK11 3LW, UK
UKHW060115300726
14090UKWH00002B/204
9781736595114